HOW DO WE MEASURE WEATHER?

by Nancy Dickmann

PEBBLE
a capstone imprint

Pebble is published by Capstone,
1710 Roe Crest Drive, North Mankato, Minnesota 56003
www.capstonepub.com

Library of Congress Cataloging-in-Publication data is available on the Library of Congress website.
ISBN: 978-1-9771-3347-2 (library binding)
ISBN: 978-1-9771-3341-0 (paperback)
ISBN: 978-1-9771-5437-8 (eBook PDF)

Summary: How fast is the wind blowing? How much moisture is in the air? Meteorologists measure weather conditions to help answer these and other questions. Learn about the tools and systems they use. Find out how these measurements help people plan their days and prepare for any weather.

Editorial Credits

Editor: Mandy Robbins; Designer: Heidi Thompson; Media Researcher: Tracy Cummins; Production Specialist: Katy LaVigne

Photo Credits

agefotostock: Erich Teister, 29; Alamy: Derek Gale, 18, Michael Ventura, 27, Ryan McGinnis, 26; iStockphoto: FatCamera, 4; Shutterstock: aapsky, 23, Aleksey Fefelov, 16, Andrey Armyagov, 10–11, Barry Blackburn, 24, Budimir Jevtic, 6, Dario Lo Presti, 21, Edward Haylan, 9, Guitar Studio, 8, Images By Kenny, 7, James McDowall, 28, Jeff Gammons StormVisuals, 14, John D Sirlin, 22, Kingcraft, 20, lavizzara, cover, 1, Makhnach_S, design element, Mimadeo, 5, Oliver Foerstner, 19, petroleum man, 15, S.Borisov, 12, txking, 13, Wattanasit Chunopas, 17, Wollertz, 25

Printed and bound in the USA. PO#3837

TABLE OF CONTENTS

Words in **bold** are in the glossary.

WHAT IS WEATHER?

Weather means the conditions in the air around us. Is it hot or cold? Is it foggy or windy? Is it sunny or rainy? These are all types of weather.

Weather is not always the same. It often changes. It may rain one day. The next day the weather may be dry. It may turn rainy again a few days later.

WHY MEASURE?

It is easy to feel if it is warm or cold. You can see if it is raining too. But we also use tools to measure weather. We find out exactly how hot or cold it is. We measure how much rain falls.

A farmer measures the rainfall with a tool called a rain gauge.

Meteorologists are people who study the weather. They use weather measurements from around the world. They try to figure out how the weather will change. They make forecasts.

MEASURING TOOLS

We use tools to measure weather. There are many kinds of tools. Each one measures something different. Weather stations have many of these tools. These stations are all around the world.

weather station

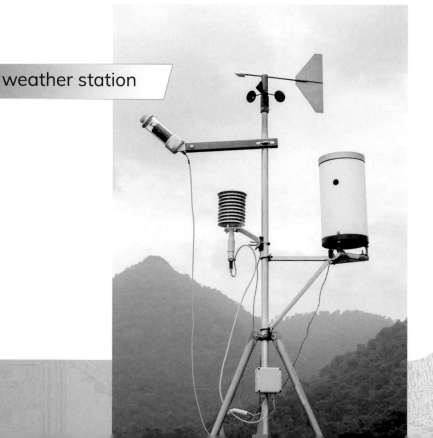

The weather is different high up in the air. Meteorologists measure this too. They use weather balloons. The balloons rise high into the sky. They carry measuring tools. They send information back to the ground.

weather balloon

Satellites can even put weather stations in space! Satellites travel around Earth. They do many different jobs. Some of them measure weather. They send information back to people on the ground.

A satellite can see a huge area. It can track clouds and storms. Satellites have many tools. They take pictures. They track lightning. Satellites help us **predict** weather.

MEASURING THE AIR

The sun heats Earth. Some areas heat up more than others. **Temperature** describes how hot or cold the air is. A **thermometer** measures temperature.

Some thermometers have a glass tube. There is liquid inside. When the liquid heats up, it rises up the tube. There are numbers and markings on the tube. They show the temperature.

Air feels empty, but it isn't. It has weight. It presses down on the land below it. This is called air pressure. It can be high in some places. It can be low in others.

Air pressure affects the weather. High pressure often brings clear weather. Low pressure can bring storms.

It is important to measure air pressure. Tools called **barometers** do this. Some have a glass tube. Others have high-tech **sensors**.

barometer

The air is always moving. This is called wind. Sometimes wind moves gently. Other times, it blows fast and strong. The wind can blow storms from one place to another. Meteorologists track wind.

anemometer

One tool for tracking wind is called a wind vane. It shows the direction that the wind is blowing. A tool called an **anemometer** measures the wind's speed. It usually has spinning cups. The faster the wind, the faster the cups spin.

MEASURING WATER

Air is made up of gases. One of the gases is **water vapor**. It is a form of water. But it is a gas, not a liquid. This gas is invisible. Water vapor in the air is called humidity. Tools called **hygrometers** measure humidity.

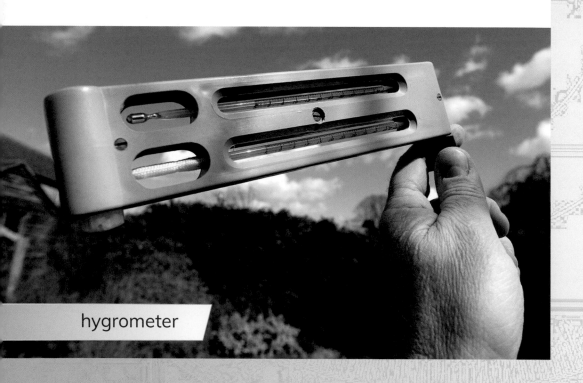

hygrometer

Sometimes there is very little vapor in the air. Other times there is a lot. There can be too much for the air to hold. Then extra water falls as rain or snow.

Clouds hold water vapor. They affect the weather as they float in the sky. When clouds block the sun, the air gets cooler. When air cools, the clouds can't hold as much water. Then water falls as rain or snow.

There are different types of clouds. Some are thin and wispy. Others are puffy. Some are very tall. These clouds can bring thunderstorms. Meteorologists pay attention to the kinds of clouds that are in the air.

How cloudy is the sky? We can see this without tools. Is the whole sky filled with clouds? Is about half the sky covered? Or are there no clouds at all?

Satellites can measure cloud cover too. They can tell what kinds of clouds there are. They measure the height of clouds. They can even tell how much water is in the clouds.

Sometimes rain falls lightly. Other times, it pours down. A tool called a rain gauge measures rainfall. It has a container to collect rain. Most have markings on the side. They show how much rain has fallen.

Some rain gauges have little cups inside. When they are full, they tip over. Then they start filling again. These tools show how fast the rain is falling.

SNOW

When air is cold, water falls from the sky as snow. You can use a ruler to measure how deep it is. But some snow melts when it hits the ground. Snow also blows into drifts. Some areas are deeper than others. Getting a clear measurement for snow is tricky.

PUTTING IT ALL TOGETHER

People measure wind, air pressure, rain, temperature, and more. Weather stations send reports from all over the world. All the information gets put into computers. Weather computers are fast and powerful.

The computers run **programs**. They know how weather works. Weather in one area might affect another place. The programs predict how the weather will change. They make forecasts.

It is important to measure weather. Doing this helps us predict storms. But it also shows us how the **climate** is changing. Is the planet getting warmer? Is it wetter or drier? Are winds and storms growing stronger?

soil samples

People have records of past weather. We also know about the climate thousands of years ago. There are clues in ice and soil. We compare today's climate to the past. This shows how it has changed.

WEATHER AND CLIMATE

Weather describes the conditions over a short period of time. It can change quickly. Climate is the normal pattern of weather over a long period of time. Different areas have different climates. Climate changes are usually slow.

GLOSSARY

anemometer (an-i-MOM-uh-tur)—a scientific instrument used to measure the wind's speed

barometer (buh-ROM-uh-tur)—a tool that measures changes in air pressure and shows how weather may change

climate (KLY-muht)—the normal weather patterns over a long period of time in one place

forecast (FOR-kast)—to predict future changes in the weather

hygrometer (hy-GRAH-muh-tur)—a tool for measuring the moisture in the air

meteorologist (mee-tee-ur-AWL-uh-jist)—a person who studies and predicts the weather

predict (pri-DIKT)—to make an educated guess about what will happen in the future

program (PROH-gram)—a series of step-by-step instructions that tells a computer what to do

satellite (SAT-uh-lite)—a spacecraft that circles Earth; satellites gather and send information to Earth

sensor (SEN-sur)—an instrument that detects physical changes in the environment

temperature (TEM-pur-uh-chur)—the measure of how hot or cold something is

thermometer (thur-MOM-uh-tur)—a tool that measures temperature

water vapor (WAH-tur VAY-pur)—water in gas form

READ MORE

Linde, Barbara M. *Makerspace Projects for Measuring the Weather.* New York: PowerKids Press, 2021.

Roberts, Abigail B. *Using a Thermometer.* New York: Gareth Stevens, 2017.

Schuh, Mari. *Measuring the Weather.* Vero Beach, FL: Rourke Educational Media, 2020.

INTERNET SITES

How Do We Measure the Weather?
metoffice.gov.uk/weather/learn-about/met-office-for-schools/other-content/other-resources/how-to-measure-the-weather

Learn Science and Safety
weather.gov/owlie/

Weather Forecasting
dkfindout.com/uk/earth/weather/weather-forecasting/

INDEX